ALSO BY SHARON OLDS

Satan Says

The Dead and the Living

The Gold Cell

The Father

The Wellspring

Blood, Tin, Straw

The Unswept Room

The Unswept Room

Sharon Olds

New York   Alfred A. Knopf   2002

THIS IS A BORZOI BOOK
PUBLISHED BY ALFRED A. KNOPF

www.aaknopf.com

Knopf, Borzoi Books, and the colophon are registered trademarks of Random House, Inc.

The epigraph is from "Shooting Script" (II, 14), *The Will to Change* (W. W. Norton & Co., New York, 1971), by Adrienne Rich, and is quoted by permission of the publisher.

"What did I know" in "The Headline" is in homage and thanks to Robert Hayden ("Those Winter Sundays").

Versions of "5¢ a Peek," "His Costume," and "Wonder as Wander" originally appeared in *The New Yorker.* Other poems in this work were originally published in the following publications: *Agni, The American Poetry Review, Antaeus, Bellingham Review, Field, Five Points, The Georgia Review, Green Mountains Review, Landfall* (N.Z.), *Michigan Quarterly Review, The Nation, The Paris Review, Ploughshares, Poetry, River Styx, Salmagundi, Southern Review, Stand* (England), and *TriQuarterly.*

Library of Congress Cataloging-in-Publication Data
Olds, Sharon.
    The unswept room / Sharon Olds.
        p.   cm.
ISBN 0-375-70998-3
    I. Title.
PS3565 L34 U57 2002
811'.54—dc21   2002018444

Manufactured in the United States of America
First Edition

". . . . to eat the last meal in your old neighborhood."

Adrienne Rich

Contents

Unknown

On the last morning of the summer, a little
family comes over the dune, across
the pond, and lays out their cloth, and their nutmeat
basket, the sweets and freshes cached in its
worried-forehead lattice-shell.
A quiet family, one mother one father one
toddler, around them the breath of the earth,
the surf, the massed crickets, the zinging
of matter coming through its narrow flute hole
in out of nothing, the soft swimming
of the air around them, the creaking harness of the
mute swan's shoulder,
music of the holy family on the beach,
rhythms of distant speech when the words are
rough-bouquet'd by gusts. Behind
the back of my mind, for an instant, I wonder
if this is the little family my relative
killed, when he was drunk, with his car, but I know
that the dead, at the moment of death, do not go
somewhere else, as if on vacation,
showing up in bathing suits,
unwounded—no, the work was deeply
done, thorough. The thought of the people
who loved those lost ones springs up in my mind like a
work party of love in a graveyard,
leaning over the holes in the ground,
maybe the small one in the middle as if to be
protected—but, the relative,
so many relatives in the human family
skilled in the irrevocable. If you know someone
who was there, that hour, at the burial,
could you tell them—I don't know what you could tell them.

Across the pond, the day's neighbors
open the earthen doors of the hamper.
Salt for eggs, a cup of milk.
If they should lack for something! If they would ask me!
Unless they have already asked me, and I did not know them.

1.

First Hour

That hour, I was most myself. I had shrugged
my mother slowly off, I lay there
taking my first breaths, as if
the air of the room was blowing me
like a bubble. All I had to do
was go out along the line of my gaze and back,
out and back, on gravity's silk, the
pressure of the air a caress, smelling on my
self her creamy blood. The air
was softly touching my skin and tongue,
entering me and drawing forth the little
sighs I did not know as mine.
I was not afraid. I lay in the quiet
and looked, and did the wordless thought,
my mind was getting its oxygen
direct, the rich mix by mouth.
I hated no one. I gazed and gazed,
and everything was interesting, I was
free, not yet in love, I did not
belong to anyone, I had drunk
no milk, yet—no one had
my heart. I was not very human. I did not
know there was anyone else. I lay
like a god, for an hour, then they came for me,
and took me to my mother.

Kindergarten Abecedarian

I thought what I had to do was to read
the very long word, over the chalkboard,
ab-ke*dev*-gi-*hij*-klem-*nop*-qurs-
tuv-wix-*yiz*, but what I had to do
was to look at a crescent moon-shape and to go
k k k k with my mind. It was strange,
like other things—that a very large Boy owned everything,
even a fire, where he could put you for the thoughts
in your head. Each day, I tried to read
the world, to find his name in it,
the trees bending in cursive, the bees
looping their sky script. Crescent moon
was *k-k-k*. Cereal bowl
uh-uh-uh. Cap-gun *puh-*
puh-puh. *K-k, uh-uh, puh-puh,*
kk-uhh-puhh, kk-uhh-puhh—
cup. Would God be mad? I had made
a false cup, in my mind, and although
he had made my mind, and owned it, maybe this was
not his cup, maybe he could not
put this cup in hell, and make it
scream the cup-scream. Maybe the paper
world was ours, as the actual one was his—
I was becoming a reader. For a moment I almost remember it,
when I stood back, on the other side
of the alphabet, *a*-b-*c*-d-
e-f-*g*, and took that first
step in, *h*-i-*j*-k
l-m-n-o-*p*, and stood astride
the line of the border of literacy,
q-r-*s*, *t*-u-*v*,
I would work for a life of this, I would ask
sanctuary: *w, x, y, z.*

Bible Study: 71 B.C.E.

After Marcus Licinius Crassus
defeated the army of Spartacus,
he crucified 6,000 men.
That is what the records say,
as if he drove in the 18,000
nails himself. I wonder how
he felt, that day, if he went outside
among them, if he walked that human
woods. I think he stayed in his tent
and drank, and maybe copulated,
hearing the singing being done for him,
the woodwind-tuning he was doing at one
remove, to the six-thousandth power.
And maybe he looked out, sometimes,
to see the rows of instruments,
his orchard, the earth bristling with it
as if a patch in his brain had itched
and this was his way of scratching it
directly. Maybe it gave him pleasure,
and a sense of balance, as if he had suffered,
and now had found redress for it,
and voice for it. I speak as a monster,
someone who this hour has thought at length
about Crassus, his ecstasy of feeling
nothing while so much is being
felt, his hot lightness of spirit
in being free to walk around
while others are nailed above the earth.
It may have been the happiest day
of his life. If he had suddenly cut
his hand on a wineglass, I doubt he would

have woken up to what he was doing.
It is frightening to think of him suddenly
seeing what he was, to think of him running
outside, to try to take them down,
one man to save 6,000.
If he could have lowered one,
and seen the eyes when the level of pain
dropped like a sudden soaring into pleasure,
wouldn't that have opened in him
the wild terror of understanding
the other? But then he would have had
5,999
to go. Probably it almost never
happens, that a Marcus Crassus
wakes. I think he dozed, and was roused
to his living dream, lifted the flap
and slowly looked out, at the rustling, creaking
living field—his, like an external
organ, a heart.

A Chair by the Fire

If there had been a flash fire,
that afternoon, would they have first untied me,
then carried me outside, or grabbed the chair and
carried me bow-hitched to it? It would have looked
odd on the sidewalk, two adults and two freestanding
children, and a child softly affixed,
a secret grandmother of the house. They could not
think of how else to stop me from pouring
ink on their bed, they thought I was a little
possessed. And I do look strange, eight years
old and bound, nursing-home drooler,
as if the device on my backside is a kind of
walker, an anti-walker. If they had gone
out, and a flash fire had come,
I could have simply stood up, bent forward
at a right angle, wrists at hips,
formal bow of an abject subject,
an object relation, and tittupped downstairs.
That could have been done without a fire,
I could have swung myself against a wall
and dislodged my pine saddle, but I sat
obedient. And I almost remember
the touch of matter, for those hours, wooden
touch. If there had been a conflagration,
that day, besides the tiny one
that singed a back closet in my heart,
I could have done a Joan of Arc,
or been carried—tipped, here and there,
with areas of flame, like a late maple,
winter coming—out onto the walk,
and been seen by the neighbors, Mrs. Langmaid,
Mrs. McGlenaghan, Judge MacBain,

and I might have felt like a child who had never been
allowed outside, now looking around
through my own eyes, as who I was,
seeing the curb, and the sidewalk, and the path
to the front door, and the pillar of magma
where that home had been.

5¢ a Peek

The day my class was to go to the circus,
I sidled into the bathroom, early,
and stood on tiptoe, up into the bottom
corner of the mirror, and leaned on the sink,
and slowly cut off my eyelashes
down close to the eyelid. I had no idea what I was
doing, or why, I studied the effect
—not bad, a little stark—but when I saw the effect
on my mother, not just anger, but pity
and horror, I was interested.
I think I had almost given up on being
a girl, on trying to grow up to be a woman like my mother,
I wanted to get disadopted
and go home to be the baby with the calf's head,
home to my birth mother the bearded lady,
my father the sword swallower stopped mid-swallow,
one with the sword. I had tried to act normal,
but when the inspiration came
I felt I was meant to act on it,
to look at my mom with my gaze trimmed to a seer's
and see her see me for an instant, see
her irises contract. I did not
imagine I could ever leave my mother,
mostly I *was* her, in distorted form,
but at least for that second the itsy scissors
spoke to her with their birdy beak,
skreeek, skreeek, witch whinge. And when
my lashes grew back, no thicker no thinner no
shorter no longer, my mother sat me
down, and taught me to bat them, to look
sidelong, blindly, and shudder them at seven beats a second.

Sunday Night

When the family would go to a restaurant,
my father would put his hand up a waitress's
skirt if he could—hand, wrist,
forearm. Suddenly, you couldn't see
his elbow, just the upper arm.
His teeth were wet, the whites of his eyes
wet, a man with a stump of an arm,
as if he had reached behind the night.
It was always the right arm, he wasn't
fooling. Places we had been before,
no one would serve us, unless there was a young
unwarned woman, and I never warned her.
Wooop! he would go, as if we were having
fun together. Sometimes, now,
I remember it as if he had had his
arm in up to his shoulder, his arm
to its pit in the mother, he laughed with teary
eyes, as if he was weeping with relief.
His other arm would be lying on the table—
he liked to keep it motionless, to
improve the joke, ventriloquist
with his arm up the dummy, his own shriek
coming out of her mouth. I wish I had stuck
a fork in that arm, driven the tines
deep, heard the squeak of muscle,
felt the skid on bone. I may have
met, since then, someone related
to one of the women at the True Blue
or at the Hick'ry Pit. Sometimes
I imagine my way back into the skirts
of the women my father hurt, those bells of

twilight, those sacred tented woods.
I want to sweep, tidy, stack—
whatever I can do, clean the stable
of my father's mind. Maybe undirty
my own, come to see the whole body
as blameless and lovely. I want to work off
my father's and my sins, stand
beneath the night sky with the full moon
glowing, knowing I am under the dome
of a woman who forgives me.

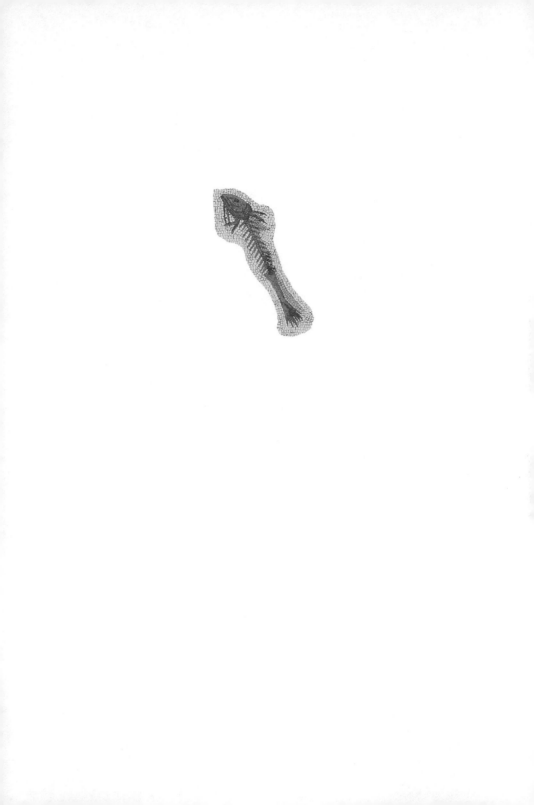

Grey Girl

for Yusef Komunyakaa and Toi Derricotte

We were walking down Park, on the grates over
the exhaust ducts of the lavish apartments,
we were walking on air, on iron bars,
three abreast—four breasts,
two on either side of the man
who had survived through various wars,
my friend and I proud to walk him through the
evening after his reading. Our skirts
faffled, we were tall, we were his color guard, his
woman of color and woman of no
color guard, we were talking about
family and race, and a greed or lust
rose in me to talk about
disliking myself. I was crouching slightly,
spider-dancing over hot air, and I
said, You want to know about white people?
I'll tell you about white people,
I lived in close proximity to them
and I *was* them, that meanness they used on me
was what I was made of. Out of the corner of my
eye, I glimpsed myself for a second
in a store window, a swirl of grey, a
thirster after substance. My companions became
quiet, as if they had pulled back,
a bit, and were holding still, with wary
courtesy. In that second, I could almost
sense myself, whuffolk amok,
one who wanted to win something
in the war of the family, to rant in the faces

of the war-struck about her home-front pain.
It is hard to see oneself as dangerous
and stupid, but what I had said was true,
the people who had hurt me most were my makers,
but there had not been what I saw now as a ring
of haters around us, encircling us.
I had a flash of knowledge of this
on the sidewalk—as we kept going, I sensed
two   living   beings, and one
half idiot, a grey girl walking. Who did she
think she was, to relish herself
for hating herself, to savor, proudly,
the luxury of hating her own people?
All evening, I looked at my friends'
womanly beauty, and manly beauty,
and the table with its wines, and meats, and fruits,
and flowers, I went back to the beginning.

2.

Still Life in Landscape

It was night, it had rained, there were pieces of cars and
half-cars strewn, it was still, and bright,
a woman was lying on the highway, on her back,
with her head curled back and tucked under her shoulders
so the back of her head touched her spine
between her shoulder-blades, her clothes
mostly accidented off, and her
leg gone, a long bone
sticking out of the stub of her thigh—
this was her abandoned matter,
my mother grabbed my head and turned it and
clamped it into her chest, between
her breasts. My father was driving—not sober
but not in this accident, we'd approached it out of
neutral twilight, broken glass
on wet black macadam, like an underlying
midnight abristle with stars. This was
the world—maybe the only one.
The dead woman was not the person
my father had recently almost run over,
who had suddenly leapt away from our family
car, jerking back from death,
she was not I, she was not my mother,
but maybe she was a model of the mortal,
the elements ranged around her on the tar—
glass, bone, metal, flesh, and the family.

His Costume

Somehow I never stopped to notice
that my father liked to dress as a woman.
He had his sign language about women
talking too much, and being stupid,
but whenever there was a costume party
he would dress like us, the tennis balls
for breasts—balls for breasts—the pageboy
blond wig, the lipstick, he would sway
his body with moves of gracefulness
as if one being could be the whole
universe, its ends curving back to come
up from behind it. Six feet, and maybe
one-eighty, one-ninety, he had the shapely
legs of a male Grable—in a short
skirt, he leaned against a bookcase pillar
nursing his fifth drink, gazing
around from inside his mascara purdah
with those salty eyes. The woman from next door
had a tail and ears, she was covered with Reynolds Wrap,
she was Kitty Foil, and my mother was in
a teeny tuxedo, but he always won
the prize. Those nights, he had a look of daring,
as if he was getting away with something,
a look of triumph, of having stolen
back. And as far as I knew, he never threw
up as a woman, or passed out, or made
those signals of scorn with his hands, just leaned,
voluptuous, at ease, deeply
present, as if sensing his full potential, crossing
over into himself, and back,
over and back.

The Given

That we would continue to be, and to be together, had about
it the unquestioned nature of a given, the tacit starting point
from which the rest of our lives proceeded.

Mark Doty, *Heaven's Coast*

Girls' dresses, then, had a sash that grew out
from each side of the waist, like an axil bud, and when we
played horses, the reins were our sashes, torn
out a lot, that feeling of standing there
holding my best friend's sash, the music of the
rip dissolving in my forearm. When she got
sick, I went to her house, after school, every
day. Sitting on her bed, I would make her
another shirt-cardboard paper doll,
reinforced at the neck and wrists with scotch
tape—and clothes for the doll, with pieces
of background showing, around the clothes:
an ice-skating costume, with some rink at the elbow; a
zoo dress, tails and ears near the tabs;
graduation gown and mortarboard,
the reds and golds of "New England" around it.
I knew that she and her mother had sprayed
their Christmas tree, in the closed garage,
a week before, with lead paint.
I didn't know that her mother was dead,
I didn't know that my friend would die
that weekend, I just made paper clothes
with backgrounds. I think I thought I could help her:
tutu, toe-shoes, riding-habit, crop
and boots, each outfit with wisps of the surrounding
scene attached to it. I can't
describe what it meant to be liked by a girl

like that—kind, and confident,
what my street looked like, with such a friend.
I did not know that she would vanish soon,
and I was not able to hold her, or kiss her,
and no one, because of the times we lived in,
could say word one, to me. A few years
later, my first sweetheart, summer camp, had that
dead-straight hair, and calm eyes.
As I held her, in my sleeping bag, I could
feel love build and build in me,
between my legs, where we were pressed together,
until my life seemed to burst, there,
like a breaking heart.

Virginal Orgy

In our Sophomore year, Solomon Wheat,
a Senior, Captain of the high school team,
carried us to the Tournament of Champions,
and we won. I left the game with my friend
the hourglass beauty, and her friend the President
of the Sophomore class. He put an arm
around each of us,
as if there were two of him, one
for her, and one for me, and I felt,
through him, linked to her long, tilted
eyes and Scythian-bow lips
and cinched waist and the large globes of her
breasts. It was almost as if I could look
into a mirror held by Mike
and see myself as Liz, the way we had
seen ourselves as Solomon Wheat.
I felt that Mike was hugging me
partly so he could hug Liz,
as if I were a moderate price
he was paying for embracing her glory. But mostly
I felt his warm, male, popular
arm around me, it was April, we were walking near
a low, flowering tree, and he steered us
into, and under, and up inside it,
and he kissed Liz, I looked into the maze
of the living stems of the wild nosegays,
and then he turned, and kissed me,
and his lips were so much bigger and more tender
than my mother's, each of his lips was larger
than her whole mouth, and the skin of his lips was like
a newborn's skin, and the flesh of his mouth,
underneath, was so liquid that each lip

seemed to be splashing like a bucket inside.
The back of my head got faint, early
Communion on an empty stomach, and that central
core, down inside me, did
the thing like a heavy gulp, with the rings
of hotness circling out. And then
he was kissing Liz, I was standing within
the standing bouquet, the orb of the tree not
estranged to me, the tightness and loose
burstness of its crowded petals
not unknown to me, and then
he kissed me again, and this time
I had forgotten my mother—this was my first
return, to him, my mouth already
wise in its hunger, feeling as if nothing
it would wish would be forbidden to it.
When he kissed Liz, I stood aside
enchanted in cherry-trance, waiting for what
was promised and would return, as if by
vow of the corporeal, the little central
throat gulping in emotion as if swallowing
tears. I would gaze into the bower, and see
the twigs and branches of our canopy,
its angles, isosceles and right, and the dropping
down of a tryst hypotenuse—
in the cone of the tree I understood
Geometry, the Trinity,
Triune Love, and the fierce tingle
of the triangle I had whirl-struck
as a child. And now I knew the kiss,
and from it the hour when the other woman

would go her way, and his other arm
would come around, like the other half
of the sky, and all the angles would close, and the
wings of the sphere open, slowly burst open.

The Wedding Vow

I did not stand at the altar, I stood
at the foot of the chancel steps, with my beloved,
and the minister stood on the top step
holding the open Bible. The church
was wood, painted ivory inside, no people—God's
stable perfectly cleaned. It was night,
spring—outside, a moat of mud,
and inside, from the rafters, flies
fell onto the open Bible, and the minister
tilted it and brushed them off. We stood
beside each other, crying slightly
with fear and awe. In truth, we had married
that first night, in bed, we had been
married by our bodies, but now we stood
in history—what our bodies had said,
mouth to mouth, we now said publicly,
gathered together, death. We stood
holding each other by the hand, yet I also
stood as if alone, for a moment,
just before the vow, though taken
years before, took. It was a vow
of the present and the future, and yet I felt it
to have some touch on the distant past
or the distant past on it, I felt
the silent, dry, crying ghost of my
parents' marriage there, somewhere
in the bright space—perhaps one of the
plummeting flies, bouncing slightly
as it hit *forsaking all others,* then was brushed
away. I felt as if I had come
to claim a promise—the sweetness I'd inferred
from their sourness; and at the same time that I had

come, congenitally unworthy, to beg.
And yet, I had been working toward this hour
all my life. And then it was time
to speak—he was offering me, no matter
what, his life. That is all I had to
do, that evening, to accept the gift
I had longed for—to say I had accepted it,
as if being asked if I breathe. Do I take?
I do. I take as he takes—we have been
practicing this. Do you bear this pleasure? I do.

The Foetus in the Voting Booth

When I swung the lever over, and the curtain
slammed shut, and I looked up,
there it was, an oval sticker
like a flat cocoon spun above the levers,
as if I were not the only living
thing in there. For a moment, I felt I could
almost understand following
the leader of the embryo,
its huge, unvarious head, its messy
beauty, the meteor-tail of its body,
its rushing in place, I could almost take it
for my god. But to make
others take it—
to sacrifice them to it—it looked archaic,
its markings those of a Pandora sphinx
or a death's-head moth. As I glanced from candidate to
candidate, in my side-gaze the foetus
looked like an eye with an uneven iris,
and its gaze seemed to be following me—
I thought that I was supposed to be
alone in the booth, the way a woman
is supposed to be alone with her body.
She doesn't have to give it to anyone anymore,
not even a child of her own conceiving.
A man has gone up the road of the air
and walked on the moon. A woman has gone
up the passage of her body to the rosy
attic of the womb, with her whisk broom,
weeping or singing—no larvum, no intricate
orb-web, no chrysalis
but she decides.

3.

The Borders

To say that she came into me,
from another world, is not true.
Nothing comes into the universe
and nothing leaves it.
My mother—I mean my daughter—did not
enter me. She began to exist
inside me, she appeared within me. And nothing
of my mother's entered me. When she lay
down with me, to say her prayers,
she was always relatively courteous,
fastidious with puritan fastidiousness,
but the barrier of my skin failed, barrier of my
body fell, barrier of spirit,
she aroused and magnetized my skin, I wanted
ardently to please her, I would say what I thought
she wanted to hear, to serve her, and so I
became a little like her, doggedly
afraid for myself. When my daughter was in me,
I felt I had a soul in me. But it was
born with her. But when she cried, one night,
a week later, such pure crying,
I made the wild grab at a vow,
claiming: I will take care of you, I will
put you first. I will not, ever,
have a daughter as I was had,
I will not ever swim in you
the way my mother swam in me and I
felt myself swum in. I will never know anyone
again the way I knew my mother,
the gates of the human fallen.

First Weeks

Those first weeks, I don't know if I knew
how to love our daughter. Her face looked crushed,
crumpled with worry—and not even
despair, but just depression, a look of
endurance. The skin of her face was finely
wrinkled, there were wisps of hair on her ears,
she looked a little like a squirrel, suspicious,
tranced. And smallish, 6.13,
wizened—she looked as if she were wincing
away from me without moving. The first
moment I had seen her, my glasses off,
in the delivery room, a blur of blood,
and blue skin, and limbs, I had known her,
upside down, and they righted her, and there
came that faint, almost sexual, wail, and her
whole body flushed rose.
When I saw her next, she was bound in cotton,
someone else had cleaned her, wiped
the inside of my body off her
and combed her hair in narrow scary
plough-lines. She was ten days early,
sleepy, the breast so engorged it stood out nearly
even with the nipple, her lips would so much as
approach it, it would hiss and spray.
In two days we took her home, she shrieked
and whimpered, like a dream of a burn victim,
and when she was quiet, she would lie there and peer, not quite
anxiously. I didn't blame her,
she'd been born to my mother's daughter. I would kneel
and gaze at her, and pity her.
All day I nursed her, all night I walked her,
and napped, and nursed, and walked her. And then,

one day, she looked at me, as if
she knew me. She lay along my forearm, fed, and
gazed at me as if remembering me,
as if she had known me, and liked me, and was getting
her memory back. When she smiled at me,
delicate rictus like a birth-pain coming,
I fell in love, I became human.

The Releasing

Then, one late afternoon,
into evening, already full
night, when he got up, my knee
still bent and resting against the wall,
I reached down for the erotic ripping-
knitting bliss of freeing myself—
and touched, first, a caduceus of hairs,
mine and maybe his, they felt dipped
in honey-glaze, and dried, I tugged at their
helix gently, and something crackled
and something tore delectably and
something broke like a cello string
sounding its furling. When I softly hooked another
crystallized hawser and it split, spitting
minute fresh kindling, and sparks of rosin, I
sensed the entry, underneath,
closing, some, and understood
that the crinked besotted sewing-threads had been
holding the gates of the body open
like the thighs of a lolling shepherdess.
Then, as I broke all the connections,
for the piercing, rough music, and the pleasure, as if
crunching a soft-shell, or stepping on a toothed
leaf in thin ice dusted with frozen
snow, I could sense the revealed creature
drawing her small cloaks around her
again, as if our planet drew
the night about her to protect our sight from
too much beauty—first half the globe,
and then the other, rests its dazzled eye.

The Clasp

She was four, he was one, it was raining, we had colds,
we had been in the apartment two weeks straight,
I grabbed her to keep her from shoving him over on his
face, again, and when I had her wrist
in my grasp I compressed it, fiercely, for a couple
of seconds, to make an impression on her,
to hurt her, our beloved firstborn, I even almost
savored the stinging sensation of the squeezing, the
expression, into her, of my anger,
"Never, never again," the righteous
chant accompanying the clasp. It happened very
fast—grab, crush, crush,
crush, release—and at the first extra
force, she swung her head, as if checking
who this was, and looked at me,
and saw me—yes, this was her mom,
her mom was doing this. Her dark,
deeply open eyes took me
in, she knew me, in the shock of the moment
she learned me. This was her mother, one of the
two whom she most loved, the two
who loved her most, near the source of love
was this.

Diaphragm Aria

It's curious and sweet to slip it out
and look inside, to see what's there,
like a treasure hunt, small toys
and dolls tucked into the root-floor of the woods,
or tilt up a stone in the yard and find,
in the groove of her path, the flame-brown newt. Now I
read the shallow cup of dregs,
shreds like clothes torn away in
eagerness—cloth of the bodies—which rips
to a cloud of threads. Here our daughter
never picked her finicky way,
here our son never somersaulted,
here only our not-children
advanced, and dropped, and surged forward
and were cut down, there a coil
of tail, here a ladyfinger, a
curl, a bone of the twin. When I have reached
into myself, and glistened out the dome,
I search its planetarium sky
for its weather, ivory nimbus, reach
of summer showers—these are the heavens
under which the grateful bodies
went to earth, dense with contentment,
moving, together, for those hour-long
moments, in a mattery paradise,
I gaze into the cumulus
of spermicide, I bless the lollers who
stay in that other sphere as we come
like surf on the shore of it.

The Hour After

The hour after, when we gaze and doze
and gaze, feels like the central hour
of my life—the joy before it may be
too enormous to be carried out
into the world. Sometimes we tell each other
things: I want to go inside
your eyes, and dwell. Last night, you held
your eyes open, long into sleep, so I could
swim and swim, I feel filled, still, with that
circumnavigation. I thank you
for your seeds, we smile, I am honored to receive them.
I love for you to know me, I whisper,
to see that knowing deep in your gaze.
Every time we open our eyes
we are married, all the time we doze
we are married—and every minute of the day
apart, married as if it could be physically demonstrated.
Early in the hour of knowing,
I had exclaimed, suddenly, kneeling between
your legs, and looking up, a moment,
It's like affection! It's very much like
extreme affection! And you'd smiled and softly
laughed. Who knows what it is like,
the play of love, foreplay, gazeplay,
dozeplay, and the play at the center like precious
work. It is like making something—
making what's there visible
and audible. We cry out, we sing,
and then for an hour it is there in the room,
the song. I look into your eyes as if I had been
parted from you for a long time or
were to be parted from you for an endless time.

What It Meant

I didn't know what it meant, that he was born
in the beauty of the lilies, maybe bulbs that had been
planted around the timbers of the stable,
or the myrrh king had brought them, or the frankincense
king. But the kings came after the birth, and he was
born in the beauty. Maybe, on the longest
night of the winter, he was somehow born
on Easter—born risen. I loved that he was
born-across-the-sea, as if born into the whole
width of the air, between here
and that magic place, the barn under
the meteor. They didn't talk about the hay,
or the water trough, or the blood, or the milk,
or the manure, with its straw-seeds inside it, but sometimes
they showed him in her arms, almost nursing,
the light around his head like a third
breast in the scene, and they said he was born
with a glory in his bosom—he had his own
bosom, as if he were his own mother
as well as his own father. And she wore
blue, always unmarked, she never wore
fleur-de-lys, and yet he was born
in the beauty of the lilies. This morning, when I looked
at a lily, just beginning to open,
its oval, slender pouch tipped
with soft, curling-back lips, and I could peek
slightly in, and see the clasping
interior, the cache of pollen,
and smell the extreme sweetness, I thought they were
shyly saying Mary's body,
he came from the blossom of a woman, he was born
in the beauty of her lily.

4.

Sunday in the Empty Nest

Slowly it strikes me how quiet it is.
It's deserted at our house. There's no one here,
no one needing anything of us,
and no one will need anything of us
for months. No one will walk into the bedroom
and ask for something. I feel like someone
abandoned—taken somewhere, and left,
some kind of resort, there's nothing for us to do
for anyone, everything is easy.
Maybe we're dead, maybe this
is heaven. After the hour in love's bed, and then
sleeping a little, we half wake
and I look, into your eyes, or into
the inner white of one eye
while the lovely lids do their wide-horizon
basking jerk, I find I can go
inhuman watching that—the single near-
simultaneous dip and rise—I for-
get the word for eyes and the concept of eyes, I just
look, an animal looking into the
liquid inside the other's head,
or through a tapered peephole into
the diorama of another dimension,
cloud, sky, pelagic water, the
sea of Eden, I am looking deep
across it, as if without knowledge, without use.

Directly

Then, one late afternoon,
I understand: the harm my father
did us is receding. I never thought
it would happen, I thought his harm was stronger than that,
like God's harm—flood, or birth without
eyes, with mounds of tissue, no retina, no
pupil, the way my father on the couch did not
seem not to be using eyes
but not to have them, or to have objects
for eyes—Jocastal dress-brooches.
But he had not been hated, so he did not hate us,
just scorned us, and it is wearing off.
My son and daughter are grown, they are well
as if by some miracle. The afternoon has a
quality of miracle, the starlings all facing
the west, his grave. I come to the window
as if to open it, and whisper,
My father's harm is fading. Then,
I think that he would be glad to hear it
directly from me,

so I come to where you are, bone
settled under the dewed tangle
of the blackish Northwoods moss like the crossroads
hair of a beloved. I come to you here
because it is home: your done-with body
broken back down into earth, holding
its solemn incapable beauty.

Frosted Elfin

When I was a child, I could look down,
over my tummy, and see myself,
classic and symmetrical,
like a slipper conch. If only I had
a flower, there, now, the brown
purple fur of a pansy ... My love sees
a flower, there, but I think of the hair,
like hair that grows in the grave, or hair
that could sprout all over the face of a daughter,
as if the mother had made of her
a weentsy bearded husband, as if a
child could catch hairiness like an illness
from the mother's whiskered nether visage.
When I close my eyes, I sense the entrance
within me like the throat of a blossom. But when I
picture it, I think of my mother.
When I was in the tub, and she took off her clothes,
that complex mark—spear in the side
and crown of thorns mashed together—
lodged a sorrow and dread in me
I had thought to take to the grave, and grow
a silver pubic beard like a sideways
Bridalveil Falls, but my love says
it is sweet beyond sweetness, it is like an oasis.
But I saw her from the tub, the bottom of the body
like the bottom of the earth. But my love says
it is a wing, a pair of wings wherein
we fly to paradise, and through it,
and to what lies beyond it. I want
to be able to look with my own eyes
and see what he sees. I will have to put my mother down a
       moment.
Just for one moment, Mom.

The Stranger

All day I had a feeling I had met someone
—someone I had wanted to meet, and been
afraid to meet, someone important, maybe
foreign, or someone I had thought dead
and then seen alive. The night before,
I had seen Jesus' bearded face
on the ceiling, within the curves of plaster
vine-coil, as if I were looking at
some modest, washed area of land
or water, or the first, clean clay—
as if I were seeing the blankness of a good
human, the desirelessness
of a grown-up parent, but it was not that . . .
Whom had I found who had been lost to me? I
could not think—and then, I remembered
the round, plump, woven-silver
mirror, which I had held, this bright
morning, between my legs, I had seen,
for the first time, myself, face to feral face.

Grown Children

One from one direction, one
from another, one day they come back, together,
and suddenly my body fits
in the air it is standing in, and my brain
fits in my skull again, and my mind
in my brain, and over the anticlines of my
mind light plays. Last week I had seen
a being on the beach I couldn't name at first,
a short, upright creature with a round
head and a swaybacked torso and brief
appendages flashing to the sides and below
like the beams of a star, so it appeared to sparkle,
to twinkle along the sand—it was a tiny
primate, and behind it along came another,
tinier and more primitive,
a dazzling winking, scintillating
along, it was a baby. And now our daughter
is asleep on the couch, not six pounds
thirteen ounces, but about my size,
her great, complex, delicate face
relaxed. And our son, last night, looking closely
at his sweetheart as they whispered for a moment, what a tender
listening look he had. We raised them
daily, I mean hourly—every minute
we were theirs, no hour went by we were not
raising them—carrying them, bearing them, lifting them
up, for the pleasure, and so they could see,
out, away from us.

If, Someday

If, someday, we had to look back
and tell the best hours of our lives,
this was one—moving my brow
and nose around, softly, in your armpit,
as if you were running a furred palm
over my face. The skin of my body
touching your body felt actively joyful,
sated yet sipping and eating. As you fell
asleep, your penis slowly caressed me,
as if you were licking me goodbye, and I lay
slack, weightless, my body floated
on fathomless happiness. When someone
knocked on the door, you didn't wake up,
and I didn't wake you, and when they knocked again
I did not rouse you, I felt sure that nothing
was wrong—it was just a someone, calling,
outside heaven, and the noise of outsideness laid a
seal on our insideness. There was just this bed,
just these two, and, passing this way
and that, from angle to angle of the room—
wall, ceiling, floor, bedpost—the
curved sound-waves of their recent cries,
by now a billion, bright webs,
look back and see this.

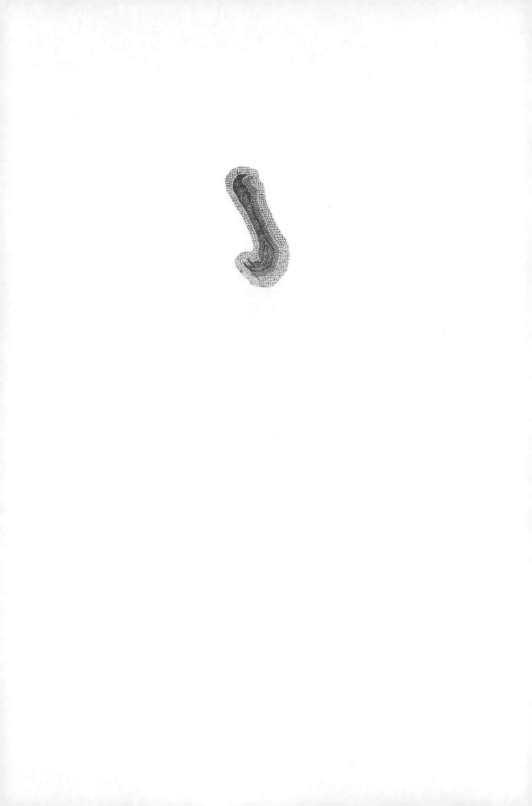

The Window

Our daughter calls me, in tears—like water
being forced, under great pressure, from densest
stone. *I am mad at you,* she whispers.
You said in a poem that you're a survivor,
that's O.K., but you said that you are
a Jew, when you're not, that's so cheap. You're right,
I say, *you're so right.* Did you see the Holocaust
movie, she asks, in a stifled voice,
there's a window on the third floor of the barracks
and I know it's a little bathroom, I used it
in Poland the day I was there, and she sobs,
a sound like someone swallowing gravel.
And the rooms hadn't been dusted, it was
as if everything was left as it was,
and some of the same molecules
might be there in the room. And there were exhibit cases,
one with hair—<u>*hair.*</u> In my mind
I see the landscape, behind glass,
the human hills and mountains, the intimate
crowning of a private life
now a case of clouds, detritus,
meshes. *And there were eyeglasses,*
a huge pile of liking to read,
and of liking books, and being able to see, and
then . . . then there was a display case
of suitcases, and an Orthodox guide was
taking a tour through. She is able, while she cries,
to speak, in a small, stopped-down voice
as if a pebble could talk. *He was telling*
a big class of Bar Mitzvah boys
to look at the names on the suitcases—
some of them had believed . . . they were going . . .

on vacation, she says—or something like it,
I cannot hear each word
but sometimes just the creak of rock
on water. I do not want to ask her
to repeat. She seems to be saying she had to
leave the room, to find a place
to cry in, maybe the little bathroom,
I feel as if I am there, near her,
and am seeing, through her, the horror of the human,
as if she is transparent, holding
no gaze to herself. *There were people not
crying, just looking,* she says, then she says
so much about us is unbearable.
We talk a long time, eventually
we even laugh, we are coming back
up as if from inside the ground,
I try to tell her it was not weakness
in her, that it was love she felt,
the sanctuary of each life and the terror
and dread of our species. *Yeah yeah,* she says,
in the low voice of someone lately
the young in the nest, maybe soon the nesting one,
within her view the evidence
of the ark consumed, and no thought of herself
to distract her, nothing distracts her, not even
the breathing of her own body as she sees.

5.

Forty Years Later

When I felt the rubber band that was looped around my wrist,
I tore it off and threw it. It landed
on the bentwood chair. I looked at the chair, its
curved strut as small around
as a child's bone. I held my wrist
down along it,
I thought of the crossing of a human with a deer,
the matching of their forelimbs. I wrapped the rubber band
around the strut, and then, with my left
hand, I bound my right wrist
to the chair. I felt calm as I had not felt
for forty years, since the day my folks
sashed me to a chair—dead calm
and at home. There was nothing I should be doing,
nothing I could be doing. It was reassuring,
as if I were being touched, deeply, as
who I am. I rested my forehead
on the chair-back, and almost fell asleep
standing there. But when I lifted my free
hand, and started to free myself,
I could not do it fast enough, I
threw the band away from me
and it writhed on the floor a moment, as if
a cast skin were the true skin,
as if a condom full of living
seed could swim on its own. Though I was
alone in the apartment, I glanced to both sides to see if
anyone had seen me. I thought of my parents, whose
bodies had seemed sacrosanct—radius, femur,
tibia, fibula, an angel's bushy
sextuple wings. Whatever ugliness

was in that house, whatever meanness,
it could not be fit in them, they could not contain it.

Sleep Suite

To end up in an old hotel suite
with one's nearly-grown children, who are sleeping, is a kind
of Eden. The one in the second bed
rests her head on two pillows—I did not know that—
as she sleeps. The one on the couch, under candlewick
chenille, has here and there as he turns
the stuffed animal his sister just gave him
for his twentieth birthday. I roam in the half-
dark, getting ready for bed, I stalk
my happiness. I'm like someone from the past
allowed to come back, I am with our darlings,
they are dreaming, safe. Perhaps it's especially like
Eden since this is my native coast,
it smells something like my earliest life,
fog, plumeria, eucalyptus, it is
broken, the killership of my family—
it is stopped within me, the complex gear
that translated its motion. When I turn out the light and lie
down, I feel as if I'm at the apex
of a triangle, and then, with a Copernican
swerve, I feel that the apex is my daughter,
and then my son, I am that background figure, that
source figure the mother. We are not,
strictly speaking, mortal. We cast
beloveds into the future. I fall
asleep, briefly living forever
in the room with our son and daughter.

The Older

The older I get, the more I feel
almost beautiful—not my face, plain
puritan face, but my body. And I will be
fifty, soon, my body getting
withery and scrawny, and I like its silvery
witheriness, the skin thinning,
surface of a lake crimped by wind, ruched
wraith, a wrinkle of smoke. Yet when
I look down, I can see, sometimes,
things that if a young woman saw she would
scream, as if at a horror movie,
turned to a crone in an instant—if I lean
far enough forward, I can see the fine
birth skin of my stomach pucker
and hang, in tiny peaks, like wet stucco.
And yet I can imagine being eighty, made
entirely, on the outside, of that,
and making love with the same animal
dignity, the tunnel remaining
the inside of a raspberry bract.
Suddenly, I look young to myself
next to that eighty-year-old, I look
like her child, my flesh in its loosening drape
showing the long angles of these strange
bones like cooking-utensil handles in heaven.
When I was younger, I looked, to myself,
sometimes, like a crude drawing of a female—
the breasts, the 1940s flare of the hips—
but this greyish, dented being is cozy as
a favorite piece of clothing, she is almost
lovable, now, to me. Of course, it is
his love I am seeing, the working of his thumb

over this lucky nickel—five times
five years in his pocket. Maybe
even if I died, I would not look ugly
to him. Sometimes, now, I dance
like shirred smoke above a chimney.
Sometimes, now, I think I live
in the place where the solemn, wild drinking
of coming is done, I am not all day coming
but all day living in that place where it is done.

Fish Oil

One midnight, I got home from work
and the apartment reeked of fish boiled
in oil. All the windows were shut,
and all the doors were open—up
from the pan and spatula rose a thick
helix of cod and olive. My husband
slept. I opened the windows and shut
the doors and put the plates in the sink
and oodled Palmolive all over. The next
day I fishwifed to a friend, and she said,
Someone might live with that, and come to
savor the smell of a fry. And that evening,
I looked at my love, and who he is
touched me in the core of my heart. I sought
a bottle of extra-extra virgin,
and a recipe for sea fillet in
olive-branch juice, I filled the rooms with
swirls of finny perfume, the outlines
in the sand the early Christians drew,
the loop meaning safety, meaning me too,
I remembered my parents' frowns at any
whiff of savor outside the kitchen,
the Calvinist shudder, in that house, at the sweet
grease of life. I had come to my mate
a shocked being, agog, a salt
dab in his creel, girl in oil,
his dish. I had not known that one
could approve of someone entirely—one could
wake to the pungent day, one could awake
from the dream of judgment.

Earth Aria

When our daughter said *Mom,* in a low voice,
some background music in the restaurant,
almost too low to hear, was doing
glottal-stop riffs. Her throaty, intense
call was like the one she uses
to draw my notice to a baby. She moved
her eyes to one side, signaling me
to look, over her shoulder, at a table
where the mouth of an oldish man was moving
together with the bass-amp sounds—they were
his voice. Our daughter's eyes opened
wide, a half-second, showing ecstatic
eyeball around the iris, and the back of my
scalp relaxed, swallowing his tones
like a portion of sleep, such low notes,
reminding my spine of its ancestry
inside the earth, as if I were sinking
down through shale, slate, bedrock,
feldspar, gypsum, serpentine,
iron, descending through older and older
strata, Cambrian, Precambrian,
back before we remember, to a time
it was not possible for an elder to harm a younger.

Wonder as Wander

At dusk, on those evenings she does not go out,
my mother potters around her house.
Her daily helpers are gone, there is no one
there, no one to tell what to do,
she wanders, sometimes she talks to herself,
fondly scolding, sometimes she suddenly
throws out her arms and screams—high notes
lying here and there on the carpets
like bodies touched by a downed wire,
she journeys, she quests, she marco-polos through
the gilded gleamy loot-rooms, who is she.
I feel, now, that I do not know her,
and for all my staring, I have not seen her
—like the song she sang, when we were small,
I wonder as I wander, out under the sky,
how Jesus the Savior, was born for, to die
for poor lonely people, like you, and like I
—on the long evenings alone, when she delays
and delays her supper, walking the familiar
halls past the mirrors and night windows,
I wonder if my mother is tasting a life
beyond this life—not heaven, her late
beloved is absent, her father absent,
and her staff is absent, maybe this is earth
alone, as she had not experienced it,
as if she is one of the poor lonely people,
as if she is born to die. I hold fast
to the thought of her, wandering in her house,
a luna moth in a chambered cage.
Fifty years ago, I'd squat in her
garden, with her Red Queens, and try
to sense the fly-ways of the fairies as they kept

the pollen flowing on its local paths,
and our breaths on their course of puffs—they kept
our eyes wide with seeing what we
could see, and not seeing what we could not see.

49½

The first long month, waiting and waiting,
I fear I am pregnant. The second long month,
a clot appears, ruby-crowned
kinglet's nest. Well—that's it,
I hear myself saying, in passionless wonder.
For a moment, I picture a changing room
at an outdoor pool—cinder-block wall
and the smell of chlorine—and no one's there,
nothing's there, not a bathing cap
or a bobby pin. It is all over.
It is so quiet. There is a slight shining
like the slight shining of truth. I will die.
I am part of a long succession. I had not
longed for a baby for years, but had assumed
I might have one any time. Now I am safe,
and taste the mercy in lack. And I'm in shock,
the concrete emptiness of the damp
room. No more eggs. How can I be
myself, without any eggs? And yet
there is someone here—all along
there was a spirit here. O I am passing beyond matter
and I am still in matter! It has been so long
since I have been a being like this.
When I was in the womb, thirty
years of half-lives beaded their dew
on my inner wall. Now I have spent them,
and yet I breathe, and caper, as if
not made to be a servant only;
now the leash of use is loosened
and I will be that scrawny, avid,

slightly bearded creature, the one
past bearing, the human gone out upon its longest thread.

White Anglo-Saxon Protestant

> My twin brother swears that at age thirteen
> I'd take on anyone who called me kike . . .
> I remember putting myself to sleep . . . dreaming of Hitler,
> of firing a single shot from a foot away, one
> that would tear his face into a caricature of mine,
> tear stained, bloodied, begging for a moment's peace.
> > Philip Levine, "The Old Testament"

When Philip Levine shoots Hitler, a man
of his species, a man he says is not
absolutely unlike himself,
nor absolutely unlike the WASPs
of Detroit, who looked down on the Jews
and the Blacks of Detroit, and on everyone else,
then I kneel down, there in the kitchen,
bending over till my forehead is touching
the floor, my hands holding each other,
I am praying, for the first time since our son
was hours late, and I threw off the disguise
of not believing in a god, and I begged,
abjectly, for our boy to come home. The linoleum is
smooth—under my brow, a bulge
of the pattern, like a harrow bank in soil.
I do not think I will get up again.
I think I have found my posture for life.
What I'm seeing about myself and my people
will not be seen and stood upright with,
but I am not upright, I am bowing to the power
of other hearts. I am begging forgiveness
for the gentiles, I am begging forgiveness for myself,
I had not realized I had thought that the WASP
was the regular, the norm, everyone

else a variation on the norm,
and I had not seen that as a child of my parents
I had privately, as if luxuriously, suffered, I am
bowing to achieve some comfort, making
a human letter in Hebrew or Arabic that
says I honor who knows more than I know,
the saltier smarter heart. I came
from people who thought they were better than anybody,
no one else was quite real to them,
and among themselves they brooded over
the oldest White blood, the bluest White eye, oh I was
theirs, they had me. Until today
I had not seen I shared their vanity,
wanting to hold my head high
for any reason, to be blind to myself
and shine. Low down to the floor there is a small
wind like the one through a vineyard, down
where the root becomes the stem, and the smell
is of zinc, and slate, and tallow earth.
This is where I will live my life,
on the floor of love's vineyard, in the furrow.

6.

Her List

She   has, at breakfast, a list of things
she   thought of during the night. She wants to
say   that she killed a leapfrog, once—
put   it on a radiator,
and   it got off, and she put it back on,
and   it got off, and she put it back on
and   spread it out. She wants to tell me
she   did not cry at her mother's funeral,
she   shows me how she peered, between
the   funeral home's curtain-panels, at
the   audience, her lips squinched up,
her   eyes slitted, like a young hex.
She   wasn't sorry when her mother died,
she   and her sister just looked at each other,
and   got in her sister's car, driving half
the   night, talking and planning.
She   hunches at the breakfast table, she consults
her   list. Her mother threw her term paper
out   the window, into the rain.
Her   mother came to her classroom and told
the   other fifth graders that she was a liar.
Her   mother sat her on the toilet till she stuck—I knew that,
her   mother took her curlers out in her sleep—I knew that,
her   mother arrived two hours late
for   a party in her honor, and wouldn't let her children
eat   or drink anything, because
the   party was in *her* honor,
not   their honor. My mother's fierce
eye   narrows at me, as if
she   is furious with me—when she used to bite
her   nails, her mother tied her to the bed
and   would not let her get up to pee.
How   many times did she do that?

One, I think, my mother says,
and I look at her—she tied me up
the once. You know what this is called now, I
say, Mom? You were a little abused—
not badly, but a little abused.
She laughs without pleasure, she looks at me with-
out delight or sorrow, she says, I never thought of that. And I
put my arms around her, stroke
the hardish lump on her back, her permanented
wee head feels too close to my breast—
but if she tries anything, I think wildly, it would
not be hard to break her wrist. I
pet her cartilaginous hump,
she was a child, she arrived without having harmed anyone.
She had formed in darkness, inside her mother, in
the liquid her mother had never touched
and had little to do with. She formed in pallor,
the shapes of what would be her breasts
and womb swimming, free, through her body,
toward their place of mooring.

Herbal Wrap

When they covered me with sheets just boiled
in sage, and tucked me in with a lead-lined
blanket, I felt afraid, and to steady
myself I thought of my husband. And his face
seemed like a mule-deer's face, the eyes
far apart, and mild, the expression
languageless, maybe almost
conceptless, as if morals are not
needed here, he looks in a state
of natural goodness. And then I thought,
his face is more like an Indian-moon moth,
the grey-green markings of his eyes. And then—
almost unconscious, in the spirit of boiled
sage—I thought, his face is like an ivory
violet, with grey-green stains, or like granite
streaked with quartz porphyry . . .
Maybe I did not want a human.
Maybe after my father and mother
I wanted another species, I wanted
to sink down—animal, vegetable,
mineral. I don't sense, in him,
the will to change me or dislike me, he seems like
a bed of heal-all, I lie down, in him,
and sleep. Or not
sleep—and no touch
is the same with him as any touch has been,
and I feel at home in him, and of him,
as if, by now, I am a part of him, I've seen
bumblebees like parts of the blossoms
they were browsing, legs dangling, I have seen
babies carried on a hip asleep,
full pitchers carried by shepherds
in the desert, full pitchers of stars

carried across the sky, or visions
of them—ideal stars, ideal sky.

Pansy Glossary

Love-in-Idleness, Tickle-My-Fancy,
Heartsease, Kiss-Her-in-the-Buttery,
when I hear the pet names of the pansy
I think I may have to go back to being
in love with my mother. She grew them, huge
and furry-faced, maybe she brushed them,
in her sleep, with some holy, baby hairbrush,
the motionless animals she loved. And she had one,
at the center of her body, and she showed it to me,
and I could not touch it, and I could not touch
my own bald bloom—from nine months on
she struck the hand that strayed toward common paradise—
I was forty before I could bear the slow
touching, there—one night, I don't
know why, fear flamed into ecstasy,
woken by his grazing stroke
to a pleasure full of awe and yet
the ordinary daily bliss of earth.
And I thought that maybe I ought to be grateful
to my mother for the late freshness of this
particular pleasure,
first she bore me, then she showed me
her Cupid's-Flower, her Kiss-Me-Quick, her
Call-Me-to-You, then she stopped me down,
and desire built—but maybe I do not have to
thank my mother. She taught me what
she knew. I am in a bouquet with her
and her mother, and her mother's mother,
my stem goes down into an underground river,
and above the grass my bodylet wanders,
grazes, sings: Constancy,
Kit-Run-in-the-Fields.

The Headline

In the medicine aisle, I saw the headline,
the father lost, and was the murder of the father
connected to the son. I kneeled down.
To believe his father might have died because of
him? The door to where he'd come from shut
behind him—almost as if it were better
he had not been born? I felt a furnace
in my lungs, as if for him. Now,
would his gift die, how could he fly through the
air among the others, slipping between them like the
freest being on earth? Because
I have felt I have harmed my family, I half believed it,
all day I prayed that from second to second
he could bear to breathe. What did I know,
what did I know. Toward evening, I saw that I had
never understood what he faced, I had
thought he was complete, like a seraph, as if
nothing could get hold of him, no
hope to go beyond the pale, far
gone in power, beyond reach,
out of mortal range—unlike
a young man on a vision quest,
who goes, in hunger and thirst, when adulthood
approaches, out onto the plain where his father
went before him, and his father's father,
and his father's father's father, and his father's
father's father's father's father.

The Shyness

Then, when we were joined, I became
shyer. I became completed, joyful,
and shyer. I may have shone more, reflected
more, and from deep inside there rose
some glow passing steadily through me, but I was not
playing, now, I felt like someone
small, in a raftered church, or in
a cathedral, the vaulted spaces of the body
like a sacred woods. I was quiet when my throat was not
making those iron, orbital, rusted,
coming noises at the hinge of matter and
whatever is not matter. He takes me into
ending after ending like another world at the
center of this one, and then, if he begins to
end when I am resting I feel awe, I almost feel
fear, sometimes for a moment I feel
I should not move, or make a sound, as
if he is alone, now,
howling in the wilderness,
and yet I know we are in this place
together. I thought, now is the moment
I could become more loving, and my hands moved shyly
over him, secret as heaven,
and my mouth spoke, and in my beloved's
voice, by the bones of my head, the fields
groaned, and then I joined him again,
not shy, not bold, released, entering
the true home, where the trees bend down along the
ground and yet stand, then we lay together
panting, as if saved from some disaster, and for ceaseless
instants, it came to pass what I have
heard about, it came to me

that I did not know I was separate
from this man, I did not know I was lonely.

April, New Hampshire

for Jane Kenyon and Donald Hall

Outside their door, a tiny narcissus
had come up through the leaf-mold. In the living room,
the old butterscotch collie let me
get my hand into the folds
of the mammal, and knead it. Inside their room
Don said, *This is it—this is where
we lived and died.* To the center of the dark
painted headboard—sleigh of beauty,
sleigh of night—there was an angel affixed
as if bound to it, with her wings open.
The bed spoke, as if to itself,
it sang. The whole room sang,
and the house, and the curve of the hill, like the curve between
a throat and a shoulder, sang, in praising
grief, and the ground, almost, rang,
hollowed-out bell waiting for its tongue
to be lowered in. At the grave site,
next to the huge, smoothed, beveled,
felled, oak home, like the bole
of a Druid *duir*—inside it what comes not
close to being like who she was—
he stood, beside, in a long silence,
minutes, like the seething harness-creaking
when the water of a full watering is feeding
down into the ground, and he looked at us,
at each one, and he seemed not just
a person seeing people, he looked
almost another species, an eagle
gazing at eagles, fierce, intent,
wordless, eyelidless, seeing each one,

seeing deep
into each—
miles, years—he seemed to be Jane,
looking at us for the last time
on earth.

The Untangling

Detritus, in uncorrected
nature, in streambeds or on wood floors,
I have wanted to untangle, soft talon
of moss from twig, rabbit hair
from thorn from down. Often they come
in patches, little mattednesses,
I want to part their parts, trillium-
spadix, mouse-fur, chokecherry-needle,
granite-chip, I want to unbind them and
restore them to their living forms—I am
a housewife of conifer tidepools, a parent who would
lift parents up off children, lissome
serpent of my mother's hair discoiled
from within my ear, wall of her tear with-
drawn Red-brown Sea from my hair—she to be
she; I, I. I love
to not know
what is my beloved
and what is I, I love for my I
to die, leaving the slack one, bliss-
pacified, to sleep with him
and wake, and sleep, rageless. Limb
by limb by lip by lip by sex by
sparkle of salt we part, hour by
hour we disentangle and dry,
and then, I relish to reach down
to that living nest that love has woven
bits of feather, and kiss-fleck, and
vitreous floater, and mica-glint, and no
snakeskin into, nectar-caulk and the
solder of sperm and semen dried
to delicate frog-clasps, which I break, gently,

groaning, and the world of the sole one unfastens
up, a lip folded back on itself
unfurls, murmurs, the postilion hairs
crackle, and the thin glaze overall—
goldish as the pressed brooch
of mucus that quivered upright on my father's
tongue at death—crazes and shatters,
the garden tendrils out in its rows
and furrows, quaint, dented, archaic,
sweet of all perfume, pansy, peony,
dusk, starry, inviolate.

The Learner

When my mother tells me she has found her late husband's
flag in the attic, and put it up,
over the front door, for her party,
her voice on the phone is steady with the truth
of yearning, she sounds like a soldier who has known
no other life. For a moment I forget
the fierce one who raised me. We talk about her sweetheart,
how she took such perfect care of him
after his strokes. *And when the cancer came,*
it was BLACK, she says, *and then it was WHITE.*
—What? What do you mean? *—It was BLACK, it was*
cancer, it was terrible,
but he did not know to be afraid, and then it
took him mercifully, it was WHITE.
—Mom, I say, breaking a cold
sweat. *Could I say something, and you not*
get mad? Silence. I have never said anything
to question her. I'm shaking so the phone
is beating on my jaw. *Yes . . . —Mom,*
people have kind of stopped saying that, BLACK for bad,
WHITE for good. —Well, I'M not a racist,
she says, with some of the rich, almost sly
pride I have heard in myself. *Well I think*
everyone is, Mom, but that's not
the point—if someone Black heard you,
how would they feel? —But no one Black
is here! she cries, and I say, *Well then think of me*
as Black. It's quiet, then I say *It's like some of the*
things the kids are always telling me now,
"Mom, nobody says that any
more." And my mother says, in a soft
voice, with the timing of a dream, *I'll never*
say that any more. And then, a little

anguished, *I PROMISE you that I'll never*
say it again. —Oh, Mom, I say, *don't*
promise me, who am I,
you're doing so well, you're an amazing learner,
and that is when, from inside my mother,
the mother of my heart speaks to me,
the one under the coloratura,
the alto, the woman under the child—who lay
under, waiting, all my life,
to speak—her low voice, slowly
undulating, like the flag of her love,
she says, *Before,   I,   die,   I am,   learning,*
things,   I never,   thought,   I'd know,   I am so
fortunate. And then *They are things*
I would not,   have learned,   if he,   had lived,
but I cannot,   be glad,   he died,   and then
the sound of quiet crying, as if
I hear, near a clearing, a spirit of mourning
bathing herself, and singing.

7.

Mother

Whatever she was to me, she was
the human caught in something she could hardly
bear, she was like a flying keening
being, limed and jessed, a small
soprano of the trees, of *ngetal* and *luis*,
reed and quickbeam. No one said
I had come from inside her, yet from where else but that
green music, and at birth I had stepped
somehow back, out of the laurel into
which I had rushed away from my father,
and my mother was a kind of sister, in thrall
to three fathers—mine, and hers,
and Our Heavenly. What she took from me
she needed, and much of what I had
I had of her gift. And it was as if I had
known her from long before, from any
town square, back to near
our beginning, as if, in her, I met
every woman burned with *ruis*,
coll, uath, saille, duir,
beth, fearn, nion—elder,
hazel, hawthorn, willow, oak,
alder, ash. When I look back,
I see her in woods, woods in flower,
although when I knew her she was doing her time
in the live grave, she ate what she could,
coloratura lips pursed
around some smaller spirit,

but if I sing, I sing from her.
First I would hear the note struck

on the piano, then her voice, scooping up toward it,
Druid mother I would hold now in my boughs and she pour
forth a newborn's caroling.

Heaven to Be

When I'd picture my death, I would be lying on my back,
and my spirit would rise to my belly-skin and out
like a sheet of wax paper the shape of a girl, furl
over from supine to prone and like the djinn's
carpet begin to fly, low,
over our planet—heaven to be
unhurtable, and able to see without
cease or stint or stopperage,
to lie on the air, and look, and look,
not so different from my life, I would be
sheer with an almost not sore loneness,
looking at the earth as if seeing the earth
were my version of having a soul. But then
I could see my beloved, sort of standing
beside a kind of door in the sky—
not the door to the constellations,
to the pentangles, and borealis,
but a small flap at the bottom of the door in the
sky, like a little cat-door in the door,
through which is nothing. And he is saying to me that he must
go, now, it is time. And he does not
ask me to go with him, but I feel
he would like me with him. And I do not think
it is a living nothing, where nonbeings
can make a kind of unearthly love, I
think it's the nothing kind of nothing, I think
we go through the door and vanish together.
What depth of joy to take his arm,
pressing it against my breast
as lovers do in a formal walk,
and take that step.

7 a.m.

Between the open bathroom door
and the frame, in that tall thin slot of air,
early in the morning I saw my mother's
winter nightie ripple like a witch's.
For a long time she was hidden behind
the wide door, then she glided out,
hunched, miniature, eighty-nine pounds, in
creamy bluish flannel, on her fingers
the sapphires she forgot to take off for bed.
She came over to me and puckered up her mouth
to be kissed good morning. This is the woman who
hit me—she was always a great kisser,
swoonlike and intense. She sits in the chair
beside me, swings her dainty legs,
gazes at me with tender hunger.
I give her a field guide to Western birds,
and she screams, she cannot believe she's receiving
all these species, and in color! She says
she's beginning to understand: there's the moon
and poetry; and now there are birds
and poetry—there's the moon, and birds,
and poetry, and Share. She says,
again, how she did not know it was me
she carried, how could she? How could she know
how proud she would be? Not *proud*, as if it had
anything to do with *her* . . .
This is the one who took me shopping
for clothes in vertical stripes, for the—uh,
size problem; we'd come back with a nice jail
shirt for me, and some ruffled outfits like a
baby layette for her. She swings her
feet and gazes at me. You have the most

beautiful mouth, she says, it is so
womanly and kind. And the most magnificent
chin, so strong, and yet soft. And then
she shows me what it was like to hit
that High C, effortlessly, in
1934, flinging up
her arms in a victory sign. Her pupilless
medicated eyes are milky blue
as a seer's. I watch her intently: my mother
is a seer. I'm a seer's daughter—there is
music, and the moon, and birds, and poetry, and my mother.

Chamber Thicket

As we sat at the feet of the string quartet,
in their living room, on a winter night,
through the hardwood floor spurts and gulps
and tips and shudders came up, and the candle-scent
air was thick-alive with pearwood,
ebony, spruce, poplar, and horse
howled, and cat-in-heat skreeled—and then, when the
Grösse Fugue was around us, under us,
over us, in us, I felt I was hearing
the genes of my birth-family, pulled, keening
and grieving and scathing, along each other,
scraping and craving, I felt myself held in that
woods of hating longing, and I knew
and knew myself, and my parents, and their parents,
there—and then, at a distance, I sensed,
as if it were thirty years ago,
a being, far off yet, oblique-approaching,
straying toward, and then not toward,
and then toward this place, like a wandering herdsman
or lamb, my husband. And I almost wanted
to warn him away, to call out to him
to go back whence he came, into some easier life,
but his beauty was too moving to me,
and I wanted too much to not be alone, in the
covert, anymore, and so I prayed him
come to me, I bid him hasten, and good welcome.

The Music

When I first stand up to my mother, when I am
fifty—and on a civic issue—
she changes, as if she's been waiting for someone
to lead her. She does not mention the beauty
of her blue eyes, but says she has been sorting
her late sweetheart's clothes—*and it BREAKS
my HEART*, she cries out. And then she cries,
as if she has been lowered down into
a river of music. *I'm not unhappy,*
she says, *this is better for me than church,*
her voice through tears like the low singing
of a watered plant long not watered—
and now it can be heard, her fear
of tears, as if they might take her far back
to something like the swimming of the flayed
in the flay. Now she lets me hear
the music of her self—I could be in a
cradle by the western shore of a sea, she could
be a young or an ancient mother.
Now I hear the melody
of the one bound to the mast. It had little
to do with me, her life, which lay
on my life, it was not really human life
but chemical, and approximate landscape,
trenches and reaches, maybe it
was ordinary human life.
Now my mother sounds like me,
the way I sound to myself—one
who doesn't know, who fails and hopes.
And I feel, now, that I had wanted never to stop blaming her,
like eating shelled animals
at midmolt. But now my mother

is like a bitty, shucked crier
in a tide-pool, which lies, beside my hand,
a lightly rocking cradle. I think
I had thought I would falter if I forgave my mother,
as if, then, I would lose her—and I do feel
lonely, now, to sense her beside me,
somewhere, in some night body of water,
as if she is only a sister. And yet,
though I hear her sighs close by my ear,
my mother is before me, somewhere, at a distance,
maybe near the end of her life,
the shore of the eternal—she is solitary,
when I hear her voice I hear the sound
of a woman alone, out ahead
of everyone I know, scout of the mortal, heart
breaking into solo.

A Time of Passion

Then we entered a time of passion so
extreme it was almost calm, the body
doubling what it wanted to bear. Anguish
and pleasure played each other. We went off what I had
thought was the path, and came easily back.
And all was done in quiet light, as if our
childhood dreams were awakened, the old
balances of power naked in the room,
the occasional smack of extreme sweet lust
struck. When I heard myself asking for things,
my low whisper was like the hiss
of some other creature. Sex had been
like music, high and bright as the moon,
sugar as the milk that had leaped in a little
arc from the breast. We had seemed to be undone
as fire may be undone from earth,
or air from water, to be blossoms the seasons
opened and closed, we had been played. Now
we were two people, playing each other,
as if there had been no sacred. Now,
will entered, and abandonment of heaven,
and extremes of feeling I had not known existed
outside of rooms where people hurt each other.
We loved each other. Our nest had been empty
some years. Locked together, or one
finger of one   touching one
nipple of the other, we were flying head
first into the earth and out, as if practicing.
It never crossed my mind that he no longer
loved me, that we had left the realm of love.

The Tending

My parents did not consider it, for me,
yet I can see myself in the woods of some other
world, with the aborted. It is early evening,
the air is ashen as if from funeral-home
chimneys, and there are beginnings of people
almost growing—but not changing—on stalks,
some in cloaks, or lady's-slippers,
others on little trellises.
Maybe I am one of the gardeners here,
we water them with salt water.
I recall the girl who had a curl
right in the middle of her forehead,
when she was good she was very very good, I was not like that,
when she was bad she was horrid, I am here
as if in a garden of the horrid—I move
and tend, by attention, to the rows, I think of
Mary Mary Quite Contrary
and feel I am seeing the silver bells
set down clapperless, the cockleshells
with the cockles eaten. And yet this is
a holy woods. When I think of the house
I came to, and the houses these brothers and sisters
might have come to, and what they might have
done with what was done there,
I wonder if some, here, have done,
by their early deaths, a boon of absence
to someone in the world. So I tend them, I hate
for them to remain thankless. I do not
sing to them—their lullaby
long complete,
I just walk, as if this were a kind of home,
a mothers' and fathers' place, and I am

among the sung who will not sing,
the harmed who will not harm.

8.

Acadia, Late

When her doctor sees another spot,
maybe malignant, on my mother's face,
he snips off the tip of her nose, and then
browses along her jaws where the first
delicate stick grew—the lady's
face is sprouting twigs, she is
a dryad who goes back, she is approaching matter
to pass through its shimmer again, its fissured
bark, and return. This is the druid
who groaned in the home, who chanted in the human,
now she is branching out, toward evening,
her limbs bent and her stems and buds coming
through as if on a bough severely
espaliered. She is thickening, part
deadwood—someday windfall. I want
to argue against the cessation of her breath,
this woody one like a little teabag,
this sylvan crone losing her outlines,
belling like an arbor. Of course I am in love with her,
the old nymph, with her old arousal, her
coppice pollen. I am one of the worker bees
around her, or a drone dreaming of being
the apple tree in full-charged bloom.
And she reaches out with her childish face
itself, with its surface, her skin crooks tiny
forefingers. She is so legendary to me
I think she could go out on High C,
like the end of an opera. Intricate nest-face,
nest in me, let me lull in you, let me
croon you to sleep, and then croon you when we both
sleep, when I am back in the night
woods beside you.

S

The wilderness river, swollen with snowmelt,
raced by, wide and flat—
at every moment, all the water
was leaving, its horizontal column was
pulled away, whole, unending,
and then, across it, not moving downriver
but dead across, not denting the surface
or leaving a ripple of wake, the diamondback
flowed. Radiant dry, pallid
dust-golden, with sidewinding ease
it poured straight at me, and it actually had
no arms, no legs, and when it crossed the liquid,
the torrent looked like a polished floor,
and all went still, as if the eternal
moved transverse across the mortal without
touching it, the hairs raised up
all over my body, which had stopped moving and now
stood in pure attentiveness,
cold and adoring.

Past Future Imperfect

When we're lying heaped together then,
jetsam, high tide line, sometimes I'll murmur,
taking his weighty head in my hands.
Sometimes the words come from excess of fondness,
sometimes from a sudden access of emptiness,
the isolation of being a single
creature who has two bodies again.
My mouth opens as if kissing, I whisper,
Did you notice me at the pool, I was trying to show
off for you—I had slow-walked toward him,
wanting him to suffer longing,
to suffer knowledge of desire. I saw you, he says,
and though we are combers' residue,
a ripple passes through us. I take
his huge head, gently, partly by the
hair, in my palms, he is almost asleep, I
mutter, close to the dune bouquet of his
ear, Ask me to look at you,
his eyes open, with a density
like cloud-light over a quiet ocean,
Look at me, he says, and I look at him,
and we laugh, softly, a few months later
I'll think of that day, and hear us, the pair
I thought was entering fresh outskirts
of play, I'll see his tiredness
and loneliness, we had weeks left, I'll look
back and see the silence, the ignorance
moving in the air around them, while the one who
knew gathered strength, and the one who did not
know kept vigil.

Wilderness

When I lay down, for the night, on the desert,
on my back, and dozed, and my eyes opened,
my gaze rushed up, as if falling up
into the sky,
and I saw the open eye of night, all
guileless, all iris of a starshine grey,
scattered with clusters of brilliant pupils.
I gazed, and dozed, and as my eyelids lifted I would
plummet up out of the atmosphere,
plunging and gasping as if I'd missed
a stair. I would sleep, and come to, and sleep,
and every time that I opened my eyes
I fell up deep into the universe.
It looked crowded, hollow, intricate, elastic,
I did not feel I could really see it
because I did not know what it was
that I was seeing. When my lids parted,
there was the real—absolute,
crisp, impersonal, intimate,
benign without sweetness, I was soaring out, my
speed suddenly increasing to its speed, I was
entering another dimension, and yet
one in which I belong, as if
not only the earth while I am here, but space,
and death, and existence without me, are my home.

Psalm

Bending over, at the August table
where the summer towels are kept, putting
a stack on the bottom shelf, I felt his
kiss, in its shock of whiskers, on an inner
curve of that place I know by his knowing,
have seen with the vision of his touch. To be entered
thus, on a hip-high table piled with
sheaves of towels, bath and hand,
terrycloth eden, is to feel at one's center
a core of liquid heat as if
one is an earth. Some time later,
we were kissing in near sleep, *I think*
we did it this time, I whispered, *I think*
we're joined at the hip. He has a smile
from the heart; at this hour, I live in its light.
I gnaw very softly on his jaw, *Would you want me to*
eat you, in the Andes, in a plane crash, I murmur,
to survive? Yes. We smile. He asks,
Would you want me to eat you to survive? I would love it,
I cry out. We almost sleep, there is a series of
arms around us and between us, in sets,
touches given as if received. *Did you think*
we were going to turn into each other?, and I get
one of those smiles, as if his face
is a speckled, rubbled, sandy, satiny
cactus-flower eight inches across.
Yes, he whispers. I know he is humoring,
rote sweet-talking. A sliver of late
sun is coming through, between the curtains,
it lights the scaly surfaces
of my knuckles, its line like a needle held,
to cleanse it, above a match. I move

my wedding finger to stand in the slit
of flame. From the ring's curve there rises
a fan of borealis fur
like the first instant of sunrise. Do not
tell me this could end. Do not tell me.

The Unswept

Broken bay leaf. Olive pit.
Crab leg. Claw. Crayfish armor.
Whelk shell. Mussel shell. Dogwinkle. Snail.
Wishbone tossed unwished on. Test
of sea urchin. Chicken foot.
Wrasse skeleton. Hen head,
eye shut, beak open as if
singing in the dark. Laid down in tiny
tiles, by the rhyparographer,
each scrap has a shadow—each shadow cast
by a different light. Permanently fresh
husks of the feast! When the guest has gone,
the morsels dropped on the floor are left
as food for the dead—O my characters,
my imagined, here are some fancies of crumbs
from under love's table.

A NOTE ABOUT THE AUTHOR

Sharon Olds was born in 1942, in San Francisco, and educated at Stanford University and Columbia University. Her books are *Satan Says, The Dead and the Living, The Gold Cell, The Wellspring, The Father,* and *Blood, Tin, Straw.* She was the New York State Poet Laureate from 1998 to 2000. She teaches poetry workshops in the Graduate Creative Writing Program at New York University and was one of the founders of the NYU workshop program at Goldwater Hospital on Roosevelt Island in New York. Her work has recieved the Harriet Monroe Prize, the National Book Critics Circle Award, the Lamont Selection of the Academy of American Poets, and the San Francisco Poetry Center Award. She lives in New York City.